LEWD

Other Books by D. W. Kreger:

The Tao of Yoda: Based Upon the Tao Te Ching
by Lau Tzu

The Secret Tao: Uncovering the Hidden History and
Meaning of Lao Tzu. With a revised translation of
the Tao Te Ching.

The Einstein Connection: Ancient Myths & Scientific
Theories of an Approaching Global Cataclysm

2012 & The Mayan Prophecy of Doom: The Definitive
Guide to Mythology and Science Behind
the 2012 Prophecies.

LEWD

The Secret History of English Dirty Words

by

D. W. KREGER

Windham Everitt

Copyright ©2018

First Printing 2019

Cataloging-in-Publication-Data-on-file

ISBN: 978-0-9833099-4-9

Published by
Windham Everitt Publishing
P. O. Box 1308, Littlerock, CA 93543

Edited by Jamielly Patacsil

Digital Production through
Kindle Direct Publishing

Ptinted in the United States of America

10 9 8 7 6 5 4 3 2 1

For Jamielly, with all my love,
Thank you!

Introduction
Solution to a Mystery, Hidden in Plain Sight

Everybody knows what dirty words are. We all learn them growing up. We know they are rude, crude, and socially unacceptable. When I was young, kids got their mouths washed out with soap for using such language, or at least we were threatened with that. And, I never really questioned why these words were so dirty. They just were. They all referred to dirty things, foul things, things you don't talk about.

Even as a child, I also knew that dirty words not only referred to dirty things, but they were also a poor choice of words. That is, if you absolutely had to talk about a subject that we considered dirty, shit for instance, there was always a more polite way of saying it, if you tried. Maybe you could say feces or just poo. So, dirty words don't just refer to dirty things, but it's also a dirty way of saying it.

Over the years, people have actually put together a specific list of dirty words. The Federal Communications Commission (FCC), which regulates broadcast media in the United States, has created such a list and has revised it from time to time. It was based on this list that the comic Lenny Bruce did a famous comedy routine, in which he talked about the absurdity of getting arrested for saying certain words. Not because it's treason or slander, but just because it's impolite. He listed 9 words that he could be arrested for saying. They were ass, balls, cocksucker, cunt, fuck, mother-fucker, piss, shit, and tits.

Of course just saying any of these words on stage in a comedy routine made people giggle. That's because we all know these words, and many people use them privately, but we never hear them spoken in public. So, when someone does say them, we can't help but giggle. That's why the comedian George Carlin had such a big hit with his comedy routine called "Seven Words You Can't Say on TV", which debuted on a 1972 comedy album. He later repeated the same routine on 3 popular HBO specials, after which the routine became infamous. And, Carlin's list was taken right from Lenny Bruce's list: cocksucker, cunt, fuck, motherfucker, piss, shit, and tits.

Unfortunately, it's not really so funny. In 1964 Lenny Bruce was actually sentenced to 4 months of hard labor for saying dirty words in public. That sounds like something that would happen under Sharia law, not in the United States of America, land of free speech. Carlin got off easier; his comedy routines were performed a decade later, when the local obscenity laws were a little more permissive. Also, Carlin avoided the FCC laws since his routine was not on broadcast TV or radio. HBO is not subject to the same laws as ABC, NBC, or CBS. But Howard Stern was not so lucky.

Stern was fined a staggering 2.5 million dollars, for daring to say dirty words on broadcast radio. Just think about that. It's one thing to reprimand your 5-year-old for saying dirty words, but it's quite another matter when the federal government fines a grown man 2.5 million dollars just for using naughty words. So, this is actually not a frivolous issue, it is something that the FCC, and the broadcast TV and radio stations take very seriously.

At some point, I don't know when exactly, I became aware of something puzzling about dirty words. It struck me as odd that some words are dirty, but other words that mean exactly the same thing are perfectly okay. Excrement, that's not a word you'd want to hear over dinner. That sounds pretty vulgar to me, but it's perfectly okay to say that on TV. If you say shit, however, you can be fined thousands of dollars. Is the word shit really worse than excrement? And, if so, why? They mean the exact same thing, so why is one good and one bad? The same can be said for a lot of other dirty words.

Is tits really worse than mammary glands? As George Carlin said, the word tits sounds like it could be a snack food, like Cheese Tits, or Tater Tits. By comparison, mammary glands doesn't sound nearly as nice to me. For example, just insert it in the above snack names and you see how it sounds. Would you really want to eat Cheese Mammary Glands? Yuk!

I became more and more curious about this, so I

began doing research and I actually found some great books on the topic, but I was still left with a lot of questions. None of the books solved the mystery of why some dirty words are bad but other words that mean the exact same thing are okay.

My question was simply this: why is it that you can say defecate, fornicate, vagina, and penis on TV, and it's okay? But, you cannot say shit, fuck, cunt, or cock, even though these words mean precisely the same things. Let's be clear. They don't just have similar meanings. Each of these pairs of synonyms have precisely the same meaning. They are no more or less obscene by definition, so why are some words dirty but other words are not? If it's not really the meaning of the word that is offensive, then what is it? What is so wrong with these particular dirty words? And, why are these words considered obscene but other words, that mean exactly the same thing, are perfectly fine to say in public, on TV, or on the radio?

Maybe it's just the slang words that the banned. Perhaps any slang word meaning defecate or fornicate is considered crude, but the proper words are acceptable. No, that's not the case. It's perfectly ok to say poop or poo-poo, or caca, or doo-doo, crap or even turd. It is just shit, and shit alone, that you are prohibited by law from saying on broadcast media.

The same is true for fuck. You can say shag or boff or bag, or 'do the nasty', and it's perfectly okay. You can even say screw. Again, it's really just fuck and fuck alone that is outlawed by the federal government. That seems awfully arbitrary, doesn't it? Why are these words, and these alone, so dirty that they are literally against the law to say out loud? Meanwhile, virtually every synonym you can think of, both proper and crude slang, remain just fine and dandy to say in public, or even on TV and radio!

Finally, an odd coincidence occurred. First, I traveled to Germany, reading and speaking German as best I could while there. Most importantly, this included reading German graffiti. Then, upon returning, I watched the film Robin Hood, the original with Errol Flynn. And, right about that time I also was reading a book on the history of the English language.

These might seem like completely unrelated events, but it brought to light a certain combination of facts with a new clarity for me. This weird confluence of events actually coalesced to give me a flash of insight. Actually, the solution to our mystery was right there, hiding in plain sight the whole time.

Though no one and nothing said it explicitly, all signs pointed to one obvious conclusion. I had figured out the origin of English dirty words. I wasn't positive at first, but then I did more research. And, everything I found confirmed my hypothesis.

Eureka! I had done it. I had discovered the real story behind why some words are dirty and others are not, even when they have the exact same meaning. This is because I had found the one and only thing that all dirty words have in common, and it has little to do with their obscene meanings. As I already pointed out, there are obviously a lot of words that refer to obscene things that are not dirty at all. But, all dirty words do have something else in common, something that the other words don't have.

By the way, not only do all dirty words have something in common, but all the non-dirty synonyms also have something in common, something that dirty words don't have. It's like I have found two separate sets of words within the English dictionary that are mutually exclusive. All of them refer to obscene topics, but one is clean and the other is dirty. Ironically, it really doesn't have anything to do with obscenity.

Strangely, my discovery was not mentioned in any of the books I read about swearing. I couldn't find it anywhere. One of the better books on the history of dirty words is titled "Holy Shit: A Brief History of Swearing", by Melissa Mohr, and I found it fascinating. The book went into great detail about the history of dirty words. And, I read other similar books as well, but none of them had solved the mystery of why some dirty words are so dirty while other slang words that mean the same thing are not.

Is it possible that I and I alone had solved this mystery? The truth is, I don't think anyone else had even asked the question, much less found the answer. Melissa Mohr's book, "Holy Shit", which I thought was excellent, had listed all the information needed to solve this riddle. So, how could she not see it? But, to be fair, she wasn't even trying. She never asked the simple question: why is shit bad, but poop is okay?

So, what is the answer of why you can say fornicate but not fuck, defecate but not shit, vagina but not cunt? Well, that's a long story. In order to understand the history of English dirty words, you first need to know something about the history of the English people and their language. You also need to know how English culture and language has evolved over the last thousand years. Once you learn that, the answer is obvious.

What follows is the secret history of English dirty words.

Chapter 1

The History of the Ænglish

Long, Long ago, before the time of King Arthur, before the Middle Ages, back during the Roman times (27 BCE - 476CE), there lived a Germanic tribe in the far north of Europe, known as the Ængles, or Ænglii, in Latin. They came from an area that is now northern Germany. And, there were other related tribes from other areas in northern Europe, the Saxons from what is now central Germany, and the Jutes from what is now Denmark. We know little about them prior to the 6th century, but eventually they played a very important role in the history of England and the English Language.

In the beginning of the 6th century CE, the Roman Army had already pulled out of the island they called Britannia, which we now call Britain. The Celtic people who were left there had lived under Roman rule for centuries. They spoke Latin and lived in Roman villages, but with no army left to protect them, they were now defenseless against barbarian invaders from the continent. Finally, in the year 516 CE, it happened. There was a full-scale invasion by a group of Germanic tribes. The invasion culminated with a great and terrible battle, known as the Battle of Mount Badon. In this epic battle, the British Celts desperately fought against the barbarian invaders from across the narrow sea.

According to legend it was King Arthur who rallied the Britons that day and led them into battle. By the end of the day, the Britons had succeeded in fighting back the German hoards. According to all reports, the German tribes did not come back, and there was peace for a generation or more. This was, according to legend, the glorious time of King Arthur and Camelot.

Eventually, however, some Ængle mercenaries were actually hired to help defend Briton against the other barbarians, and this proved to be a tragic mistake. The mercenaries double-crossed the British leaders. They learned their defenses, and then they allowed their fellow Germanic tribesmen to make landfall. Along with the Saxons and Jutes, they swept through the country and eventually conquered all the land.

They set up their own country. From what we can tell, the Ængles were dominant among the tribes, and they called their new country Ængland. And, their language was Ænglish. History records these people as the Anglo-Saxons, but of course we refer to them today simply as English or Saxons. The language they spoke was what we now call Old English, but if you've ever seen it then you know it looks nothing like English. Old English was essentially a German dialect.

Germanic Languages of Northern Europe

The Germans did not only conquer Britain. Between the 5th century and the 11th century, the Germanic tribes from the East had completely conquered northern Europe. The Saxons controlled what is now Denmark and Northern Germany. The Francs conquered everything below the Rhine river and to the West, in what is now France and Normandy.

The Frisians controlled the northwest coast of Europe, in what is now Belgium and the Netherlands. And, of course, the Anglo Saxons crossed the English Channel and conquered England.

Notice that the French Celts and British Celts were both conquered by Germanic tribes. In England, they were conquered by the Anglo-Saxons. In France, it was the Francs (Franks). Of course, in England, the Ængles controlled the country and it came to be known as England and their language was English. Likewise, in France, the Francs conquered the country and it came to be known as France and their language was French.

But, there was a big difference between the Old English and Old French languages. Old English was almost entirely based on the Germanic dialect that the tribes brought with them from the continent. They seem to have all but wiped out the native Celtic languages of southern England, that we call Gallic. Almost none of the native Gallic dialects such as Iceni, Cornish, or Manx survived. But, the reverse happened in France.

When the Francs invaded what is now France, they did not wipe out the local Celtic people, their language, or their culture. In fact, there continued to be Celtic Kings and Frankish Kings ruling their respective areas. The locals, under centuries of Roman occupation, had developed a hybrid language made up of Latin and Gallic. The Frankish Kings spoke a Germanic dialect originally, but the people they ruled never adopted it, and eventually the Francs' dialect died out.

The Francs' dialect only survived in one area, in what is now Holland. We know it as Old Dutch. So, you see that Old Dutch, Old German, and Old English were all sister languages. The Francs gave the country of France its name, and hence the name of its language, but it was not the Frankish language at all. Old French was overwhelmingly Latin based, but with a lot borrowed from Gallic, especially in the pronunciation and inflection.

Hence, even though they were both conquered by Germanic tribes, Old English and Old French were vastly different languages, as different as German vs. French is today.

There was also another important language called Old Norse, which was related to the other Germanic languages. Old Norse was used by tribes in the far north, including what is now Scandinavia, Denmark, Northern Germany, northern Scotland, and northern England.

As such, many words in Old English actually originate from Old Norse. So, when it came to trade with foreign lands, they could likely all understand each other whether speaking Old English, Old German, Old Norse, Old Dutch, or some other Germanic dialect, such as Old Gutnish. And, they most likely used a Runic alphabet, as shown below.

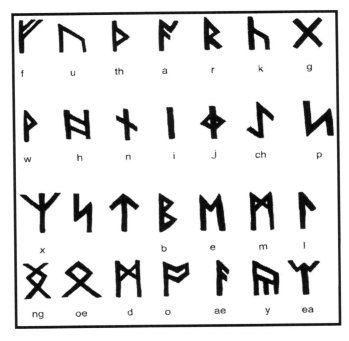

We don't have any record of what language preceded these northern European languages, but it's clear that all the above ancient languages were part of a single family of Germanic languages. It is also possible that they are all offshoots of a single Germanic language that existed many thousands of years ago. This is because, while the spelling of certain words changes a bit from language to language, many words are similar enough to be consistent across all of the above languages (see Appendix). So, we often refer to Germanic as a language group, and that includes all the above ancient languages, including Norse.

It's important to remember that the Norse influence in England was not limited to their language. All of the Germanic and Norse people shared a common cultural heritage as well. They had similar beliefs and traditions. And, prior to Christianity, they all worshipped the same Norse gods, such as Odin, Thor, and Frige.

We know these Norse gods were worshipped by pre-Christian Anglo Saxons because of how they named the days of the week. You see, the Romans named the days of the week after the sun, the moon, and the planets. And, the Anglo-Saxons borrowed this Roman system to name the days of the week as well.

Three of these are obvious, Saturn-day (Saturday), Sun-day, and Moon-day (Monday). But the others are not so obvious. They are named for Mars, Mercury, Jupiter, and Venus. And, these were not just planets, they were also Roman gods. The problem is that the Anglo-Saxons had very different gods. The Roman names meant nothing to the them.

To solve this problem, the early Anglo-Saxons substituted the Norse gods in place of the Roman gods. For instance, the Romans called Sunday 'dies Solis' because 'Solis' was the Roman name for the sun. But, the Norse sun goddess was named Sunne. So, they called it Sunday. Likewise, the Roman name for the moon was Lunae, so they called Monday 'dies Lunae'. But, the Norse moon god was named Mona, so they called the day Monday.

The other days were also named after Norse gods as well. Instead of a day named after Mars, the god of war, they named it after Tiw, the Norse god of War. Mercury's-day became Odin's-day (phonetically spelled Wodne's-day). Jupiter's-day became Thor's-day. And Venus'-day became Fri's-day, after Frige, the Norse goddess of love, marriage, and wisdom. Over the last 1500 years, the spelling has changed a bit but we still call these days by the names of the Norse gods: Tuesday, Wednesday, Thursday, and Friday. This shows the influence of the Norse culture among early Anglo-Saxons.

Conclusion

The purpose of this chapter is simply to introduce you to the first English people, and their Germanic cousins, the Saxons, Norsemen, and the Dutch. Culturally, they were all closely related, with Germanic and Norse dialects and a common Norse mythology and cultural heritage. We don't normally think of Anglo-Saxons as being German or Norse, but they absolutely were and, believe it or not, that's important for solving the mystery of dirty words.

Likewise, it is just as important to know that the people of France were not Germanic in origin, far from it. Even though their lands were conquered by the Germanic tribes of the Francs, and their language was named after the Francs, it was in name only. For the most part, the native French people retained their Latin dialect, Romanized Celtic beliefs and culture. This is important because there appears to have been some cultural conflict between the Germanic people and the French.

Remember how the British Celts feared the barbarians from across the sea, who threatened to rob them of their Roman civilization and lifestyle? Well the Romanized French Celts felt the same way about these Germanic barbarians. By the 6th century, many French people had already converted to Christianity and had been living as Romans for Centuries. Imagine how they loathed these unwashed Germanic heathens, coming into their land and bullying their people.

Even then, the French probably thought themselves superior. For hundreds of years they probably dreamed of seeking their revenge against the German barbarians. And this undoubtedly set up a potential showdown between the Germanic and French peoples of that time. Finally, such a showdown did take place in England about 1000 years ago.

We know that the language of Old English did not last forever. It was eventually replaced by Middle English. And the date when Old English ended and Middle English began is important because it gives us the next clue in solving the mystery of the origin of dirty words. We can date the end of Old English to one particular year; that year was 1066 CE. What happened in that fateful year? The Norman Conquest happened.

Chapter 2

The Norman Conquest

In the early middle ages, Normandy was part of the Carolingian dynasty, a Frankish noble family in northern France. In the year 911, after being repeatedly sacked and burned by Viking invaders from the north, King Charles the Simple invited a group of Vikings to settle there. They were given land and titles in exchange for protection against further Viking invasions. The Vikings were known as the Norseman, or Norman for short. They flourished there, and in time the land became known as Normandy.

Though the Norman people spoke Norse originally, the Norman settlers accepted the local French language and culture. So, the Norman language became
a dialect of French, a combination of Latin and Gallic. Eventually, this language became what is known
as Anglo-Norman, but it was really more French than
anything else. More importantly, the Normans' culture, attitudes, beliefs, and traditions were largely
French in origin.

King Edward the Confessor

Meanwhile, the Saxons had ruled England since
the late 6th century. In 1002 CE, King Æthelred II
of England married Emma, the sister of Richard II,
Duke of Normandy. That formed an alliance between
the two countries, England and Normandy. They had
one son together, Edward the Confessor. King Edward
became king in 1042, but he never had an heir of his
own.

Ironically, King Edward of England actually
spent most of his life in Normandy with his Mother's
family.

While in Normandy, King Edward struck up a friendship with his first cousin, once removed, William, Duke of Normandy, who was a direct descendent of the first Vikings who settled in Normandy. Unfortunately, he was a bastard, so he was also known as William the Bastard.

King Edward loved his cousin William so much that it is believed that Edward wanted William to be his successor, but if that was the case it was never written down. When King Edward died in 1066, it was not clear who would be his successor since he had no heir.

William the Bastard

The Witenagemot, a council of Saxon noblemen, convened a meeting to decide who would be the next king. They chose Harold, Earl of Wessex, King Edward's brother-in-law. But poor Harold would rule less than a year.

William knew that the Saxon Witenagemot would never pick a Norman bastard to rule England, even though he was a first cousin to the late King Edward. Feeling that he was the rightful heir to the throne, and Edward's chosen successor, he took matters into his own hands, and launched an invasion of England. On the 14th of October, 1066 AD, William the Bastard defeated and killed King Harold at the battle of Hastings. Harold was the last of the Anglo-Saxon Kings. This was known as the Norman Conquest.

While this was a war fought on the battlefield, it was also a clash of two different cultures. On the one side was the Normans with their French language and culture, and on the other side you had the Anglo-Saxons with their Germanic language and Germanic/Norse culture. In every conflict in Northern Europe since the Battle of Mount Badon, the Germanic people had never lost. But, in England, in 1066, the French finally won.

William the Bastard was forevermore known as King William I, or William the Conqueror. He was the very first of the Norman Kings. Though ruling his new kingdom would prove to be harder for William than he thought. It took years to put down one Saxon rebellion after another. William would have to be completely ruthless if he was to unify and maintain his kingdom for generations to come. And he was indeed ruthless.

William's methods were extreme. He took one fourth of all the land of England for his own personal use. He loved hunting and wanted all of the wild deer in England for himself and his fellow Norman nobles. The penalty for hunting deer on the King's land was to be blinded by having your eyes burned out, or to be mutilated in some other way. If you were lucky you would be swiftly executed. Norman courts were set up spontaneously to administer justice, but your justice depended on your ethnic background. Normans and Saxons were treated quite differently.

The number of Saxons who died at the battle of Hastings would be dwarfed by number of people who were either killed or died by starvation over the next decades. And, the more-cruel William was, the more the Saxons fought back. In Yorkshire, a Saxon stronghold, a group of Norman knights were massacred by Saxons.

After that, William became even more cruel and murderous than before. He focused his wrath on Yorkshire. Many villages and towns were burnt and locals were murdered. Their houses, crops, livestock, and farming tools were all burned to the ground. During the next winter it is estimated that over 100,000 people died of cold and starvation.

To eliminate any future rebellions organized by the Saxon nobility, the Saxon lords and dukes were robbed of their lands and titles. Many were either killed or forced to become common criminals just to survive. Eventually, there was not a single Saxon noble left in England. William was not without a conscience. He wrote the following:

"I have persecuted its (England's) native inhabitants beyond all reason. Whether gentle or simple, I have cruelly oppressed them; Many I unjustly inherited; Innumerable multitudes, especially in the county of York, perished through me by famine or the sword."

–William the Conqueror

And, King William was also well aware of the idea that absolute power corrupts absolutely. He also once said: "Unlimited power is apt to corrupt the minds of those who possess it; and this I know, my lord, that where laws end, tyranny begins." And, from what we can gather from history, his descendants continued his cruel oppression of the Saxon people where he left off.

The Story of Robin Hood

This is where the story of Robin Hood comes in. If you remember, the story of Robin Hood was set sometime after the Norman Conquest, in the late 12th century, during the time of the Plantagenet

Kings, Richard the Lionheart, and his brother Prince John, who eventually became King. But, the Plantagenet Kings were direct descendants of William the Conqueror. So, they were really all Norman Kings.

In the story, Robin Hood, a nickname meaning Robin the bandit, had once been a Saxon Nobleman named Sir Robin of Locksley. And, because of Saxon persecution by Prince John, Sir Robin had his lands and titles stolen from him, and he was forced to flee to the forest for rest of his life. While there, he organized a group of Saxon bandits, who robbed the Norman nobles as they traveled through Sherwood Forest. And, they organized raids on Norman castles and food stores in nearby Nottingham.

Some historians question whether the story of Robin Hood wasn't really just a myth. But, we know that there were real life characters similar to that of Robin Hood. One famous example was Hereward the Wake, who actually was a Saxon lord and landowner in Lincolnshire, near the Sherwood Forest. After the Norman Conquest, he fled to the forest and marshes to fight the king's oppression, and lived like a criminal for years, until he was finally caught and killed.

And, there were other similar stories. One ballad from the 13th century identified Robin Hood as the Earl of Huntingdon, who was actually a Scottish prince living during the time of King Richard the Lionheart. He was evidently not happy with how Prince John was ruling the country in the absence of King Richard. He did, in fact, lay siege to Nottingham Castle, and took the Sheriff of Nottingham captive. This very well could have been the inspiration for the story of Robin Hood.

Since the Middle Ages, there have been various stories and ballads written about this bandit known as Robin Hood. But, the defining feature of all the different stories is how cruel the Norman nobility were to the poor Saxon peasants. According to all these stories, the Normans forced the Saxons to pay such high taxes that they could not afford to live. They were literally starving to death. And, Robin Hood, a Saxon nobleman, stole from the rich and gave to the poor. From what we know of the Earl of Huntingdon, as well as King William's own admission of persecuting the Saxons, there is more than a grain of truth to this story.

They say that history is written by the victors. And, it is also during this period that English history began to be rewritten. Pre-Saxon, British Celts like King Arthur and Merlin began to be romanticized as highly civilized and Christian, which they were neither. They were, however, Romanized Celts, just like the French. Meanwhile, the early Anglo-Saxons were characterized as a heathen Saxon hoard. They were seen as crude, uncivilized, ruthless barbarians and invaders. This revision of English History is in no small part due to Norman prejudices against the Saxons.

Who were the so-called Norman Kings?

We know that the Norman Kings were brutal and cruel to the Anglo-Saxon people, even Saxon royalty. But, the history books say that the Norman Kings only ruled from 1066 to 1154. After that there was the Plantagenet Kings, and then the Tudors, the Stuarts and so on. So, is it really fair to say that the Norman anti-Saxon prejudice persisted for centuries, even during the years of the Plantagenets and the Tudors? Yes, because the Plantagenets, Tudors, Stewarts, and so on were all descendants of the Norman Kings. It was one royal family lineage.

What many people do not realize is that the current English monarchy, including Prince William and

Prince Harry, can actually trace their ancestral roots in an unbroken lineage, all the way back to William I, the leader of the Norman Conquest and the first Norman King. That means that all the Kings and Queens of England were Normans. We talk about the Plantagenets, Tudors, and so on, but each of them were really just the descendants of the Norman Kings' family lineage.

The only reason that the names changed is because when a female heir got married she took her husband's name. Then, if she or her son became the next monarch, the name of the royal family would change accordingly. The only exception was the Windsors.

35

King George V's last name was Saxe-Coburg-Gotha, and he changed the family name when they were at war with Germany because he thought it sounded too German. He took the name of their primary residence, Windsor Castle, and he became the first Windsor King.

It might look like the throne changed hands over the years, sometimes violently, or due to war. But, in reality, they were all cousins. The War of the Roses was between two rival branches of the royal house Plantagenet; the House of Lancaster, whose symbol was a red rose, and the House of York, whose symbol was a white rose. But, both families were descendants of King Edward III, a Plantagenet King.

Then there was the Tudor Kings and Queens, but they also were descendants of the Plantagenet Kings. You see, the First Tudor King and Queen came about by a marriage between a York and a Lancaster. Henry Tudor, who became King Henry VII, was a Lancastrian, and descendant of a Plantagenet King. His wife, Elizabeth of York, was the daughter of King Edward IV of the house of York. This marriage was a union between the two houses and effectively ended the War of the Roses, and literally created a new house made up of both branches of the house of Plantagenet. Hence, the Tudors were also descendants of the Norman Kings.

They were all Norman Kings. Even the current Royal Family of England, the Windsors, can trace their family tree to the Norman Kings, all the way back to William the Conqueror. It is certainly not fair to say that all of the English royalty throughout history have been anti-Saxon, but they were definitely all part of the same family. So, in the centuries after the Norman Conquest, presumably there were some attitudes and prejudices that were passed down from generation to generation.

Over the Centuries, the Normans and Saxons intermarried, and nowadays you would be hard-pressed to know which middle class English families were of Saxon descent and which were of Norman descent. But, during the centuries after the Norman conquest it was very definitely an issue that the English people were all too aware of. Even a hundred years after the Norman Conquest, it would have probably been obvious who was a Saxon and who was a Norman.

The Death of Old English

When the Norman Conquest occurred, overnight the Norman language became the official language of England. It was known as Anglo-Norman, but that is deceiving. As we said in the last Chapter, the Normans spoke a French dialect. Yes, for hundreds of years after the Norman Conquest, the official language of England was French! I bet that's something most people didn't know. And, as a result, the language of Old English became extinct.

At first, Old English was merely driven underground. It was probably still spoken by Saxons in their homes and between themselves, but the official languages used in castles, legal courts, schools, and churches was either Latin or French.

In the next hundred years after the Norman Conquest, the language of the Saxon peasants was then gradually replaced by a hybrid of English and French. This often happens in places where two languages are spoken. In southern California, along the Mexican border, many people speak what's known as Spanglish, a hybrid of English and Spanish borrowing words from both languages. This is essentially what happened among the Saxons, as their children grew up living with and working for Norman lords and ladies. This new language that replaced Old English is what we call Middle English.

At the same time, the reverse was happening among the Normans. We know that by 1190, most of the royal Norman families had to hire French tutors for their children because it simply wasn't spoken enough for them to pick it up in everyday life. All their workers and servants were Saxons. And, they probably had to learn English to be able to communicate with them. So, they too probably created their own hybrid of French and English, but it was likely very different than the common Middle English spoken by the Saxon peasants in the fields. Gradually, each language was becoming more like the other.

By the year 1400, the Norman French language in England was probably like Latin is today. People still learned it, they still used it in academic and legal settings, but it had become a dead language. Middle English was increasingly becoming the only commonly spoken language, while Latin was used in Church and for official purposes.

Two English Languages

Looking back across hundreds of years it's easy to see Middle English as a monolithic entity, one language with one vocabulary. But, that simply wasn't the case. The rich noblemen undoubtedly spoke a high-class form of Middle English, with many if not most of their vocabulary coming from French and Latin.

Meanwhile, the commoners spoke a low-class Middle English, which probably contained many

Saxon words that the Norman nobility found crude and distasteful. So, there were at least two different English dialects, separated by class and breeding, and this was probably true everywhere, in addition to any regional differences.

We know this is true for two reasons. First, we know this must have been true then because it is still true even now in England. You still have a high-class form of English spoken by the British upper crust, and this includes differences in both pronunciation and vocabulary. And, on the opposite end of the social hierarchy, you have the Cockney accent of London's East End, with their own colorful vocabulary. And, this is true today, even one hundred years after the end of the Edwardian Age (1914), at a time when everyone listens to the same BBC radio and TV.

So, English accents and vocabulary are still passed down from parent to child, generation after generation. Imagine how much more separate the two dialects of Middle English were when each group came from two different racial and ethnic backgrounds, and were more socially insulated from each other by class than today.

The second way we know that there were two separate forms of Middle English is simply by looking through the English dictionary at the origins of words. About half of English words come from Latin or French. The other half comes from the Germanic languages.

Why did the Normans use Latin words? Old French, if you remember, was created by the Celtic people living under Roman rule. What they created was really a form of Latin. And, when the Normans conquered England they brought with them many words from Old French, and most of those came from Latin originally.

Most of the other half of English words come from the Germanic languages, either Old English, Old German, Old Norse, or Old Dutch. These words come from the vocabulary of the peasant class, the Saxons and other Germanic and Norse immigrants who came to England to find work as laborers and servants.

Even though both sets of words are all mixed up in the English dictionary as though they are part of a single language, that's not really the case. In fact, these two sets of English vocabulary words actually come from two different languages, with two different ethnic and cultural histories as well. One came from the Germanic people of northern Europe, especially from the Anglo-Saxons and their language, Old English. The other came from the Normans of Northern France, and their language, Old French and Latin.

Most people are probably not aware of it, but there really are two distinct vocabularies contained in English, even though it would be hard to know which word is which without a dictionary. Nonetheless, the difference between these two vocabularies actually does affect how you come across to people.

Even today, if you use words from Old French or Latin then you might appear to be more high-class, well-educated, or well-bred. But, if you use words of Germanic origin, you might sound a bit crude, uneducated, or coarse. By using words of Germanic origin, you might appear more common. If this is true even today, imagine how much more true this was during the Middle Ages, when the culture was rife with racial and cultural prejudice between the Normans and Saxons.

Eureka!

This is it! Right here! Remember, in the introduction, I mentioned the two sets of words in the English dictionary that refer to obscene things? How one is proper and the other is dirty? Well, this directly refers to the two English dialects of Middle English, one Saxon and one Norman. So, this gives us two sets of words, both describing vulgar topics, one dirty and the other more proper.

In case you haven't guessed it already, defecate is from Latin and shit is from Old English! And, the same pattern holds true for all other dirty words and their acceptable synonyms. For instance, vagina is from Latin, and cunt is from Old Norse. Likewise, fornicate is from Latin, while fuck is definitely of Germanic origin.

So, this is it! This is the origin of dirty words. Every modern dirty word is considered low class because they all stem from the Germanic language group. Every proper word comes from the Norman language, and is either of Latin or Old French origin. So, our modern dirty words actually stem from a 1000-year-old prejudice against Saxon peasants by the Norman nobility. The fact that you can still be arrested or fined to this day for speaking Saxon vulgarities in public is the Curse of William the Bastard.

So, you might think that we are done. We've discovered what is different about the 7 words you can't say on TV. So, that's it. Our job is done, right? Not so fast. It turns out that during the Middle Ages these Saxon obscenities were not really considered dirty words at all. That is, they were no dirtier than any other Saxon words. The modern dirty words were not really banned until hundreds of years later. It turns out that it's a long and interesting story about how obscenities became *obscene*, and how lewd became *lewd*.

Chapter 3

Swearing in the Middle Ages

Our modern dirty words were not considered obscene during the Middle Ages, even in the Church. Back then swearing literally meant swearing, as in swearing an oath to God. A common swear was "God blind me", such as "God blind me if I'm lying." This is still used in in England to this day, though it's usually pronounced with the Cockney accent: "Cor, blimey!"

Similar swears were God bless me, or so help me God, as in "God bless me, I'm telling you the truth." Children would get in trouble for saying swear words, but not for saying what we consider obscenities. They would definitely get in trouble for saying "God blind me", but it was perfectly okay to say "Mom, I have to shit."

To understand this, you have to remember that in the Middle Ages, prior to the Renaissance, there was no privacy in a Medieval Hall. As in the story of Beowulf, everyone ate, slept, shit, and fucked in one big hall. Saxon servants usually slept in the same room as their Norman masters, so that they could empty the chamber pot in the middle of the night, if necessary. As such, there was no such thing as privacy and hence no such thing as shame regarding private body parts or bodily functions.

Shame at this time was a social class issue. You could not be shamed in front of your inferiors, only among your betters. So royalty could go naked in front of you and say whatever they wanted. And they did. Noble women went topless on occasion. Queen Elizabeth often wore an open robe in court, and was naked underneath. This was considered a compliment to whoever witnessed her.

The concept of obscenities didn't really exist. Feeling shame over body parts or bodily functions such as going to the toilet or having sex with your spouse was unheard of. The only shame one felt was due to bad behavior, and that was almost exclusively related to your religion and morals, or lack of it.

The key to bad words in the Middle Ages was really sin, not obscenity. So shit was not bad since it would not lead to sin. Other words such as tits and fuck were potentially bad, since they could lead to sinful thoughts. Even so, these words were routinely used by Saxon commoners, with little or no shame.

It may surprise people today but many common words at that time would be considered obscene today. Take for instance these common words in Middle English. A heron was called a shiterow. The bird we now call a kestrel was once called a windfucker, presumably because of how they hang in mid-air and thrust their tail feathers to and fro. A smartweed was called an arsesmart. The herb we call a fumitory was called a cuntehoare. A medlar tree was called an openarse, because of how the fruit opens up, resembling an anus.

There was a street in London's red light district in the 1500s called Gropecunte Lane, and that was a common street name in towns and cities in the Middle Ages. The street name simply designated that it was the prostitution district, where you could grope a cunt. A street in Warwickshire was called Shetewell Wey, presumably it was where you could find the public latrines.

As we mentioned in the last chapter, there are English words of French or Latin origin brought over by the Normans, and then there are the English words of Germanic origin. Arse, which was later spelled ass, as well as shit and fart are all Anglo-Saxon words (pre-1066). But, the other words, such as fuck and cunt, are also of Germanic and Norse origins and all quite old. Fuck was first used in English writing in 1278. And, the other dirty words are equally old or older.

What we think of as obscene words today were just common English words at that time. Though they may not have been used widely by Norman nobles, they were the common vocabulary of the Saxon peasants, as well as other German, Norse, or Dutch immigrants. In fact, among commoners there was no other word in Middle English for a vagina other than cunt. Yes, they could have used a word of French or Latin origin, such as vagina or vulva, and the Norman upper class probably did just that. But, the average Saxon peasant wouldn't use Latin words unless they were in school or church because that wasn't really part of their language.

Likewise, the word that meant defecate in Middle English was shiten, coming from the Old English word, sciten. This wasn't a bad word, it was simply how they said 'defecate'. And, the same is true for all the other modern dirty words.

Actually, the word fuck just meant to repeatedly strike or to move back and forth. The Old English word for intercourse was swive, not fuck. The Germanic word for 'repeatedly striking' only later came to mean intercourse, for obvious reasons.

This is the key. All of the words that are banned in Modern English were just common words in Middle English, but they were all of Germanic or Norse origin. That is the one thing that makes them different from all other words of a similar meaning. At the time, they were all just common English words spoken by the common Saxon peasants of England.

The Renaissance & the Birth of Shame

It was not until the Renaissance, in the late 15th and 16th centuries, that private parts and private acts became shameful in any way. The Renaissance (1500-1635 AD) brought an increased importance to etiquette and decorum, and also it brought more taboos. By the 16th century, obscenity was becoming both a moral and a social issue, creating the concept of shame.

The word obscene comes from the Latin *obscenus,* and it was not even used in English writing until 1591. This means that 'obscenity' was a Renaissance concept, unknown in the Middle Ages. It was a new word meaning foul or indecent. But, of course, it also took on the meaning of being immoral, such as committing a sin. And, just as Lenny Bruce noted, this is a bizarre concept if you think of it. Since when is going to the bathroom a sin?

"16th century people were ashamed of more things than their medieval forebears, and ashamed in front of more people. It became more and more important to conceal these various shameful body parts and actions, in public life and polite language."

-Melissa Mohr; in Holy Shit, p. 156.

The renaissance architecture introduced more individual rooms into the traditional halls and residences. And, with more physical walls, there were more psychological walls, hence more shame. People began wanting to separate themselves when they were toileting or having sex. As a result, privacy as a concept was invented. And this inevitably led to shame.

Still, obscene words were not so bad to say in public, even in the Renaissance. Shakespeare's work contained many innuendos and dirty jokes that at the time were not yet so dirty that you couldn't say them in public. These dirty jokes were probably just as humorous as dirty jokes are today.

For instance, in Shakespeare's Hamlet, Act 3, Scene 2, the young Prince Hamlet asks if he may lie in Ophelia's lap. She replies "No, my lord." He then clarifies that he meant to lay his head upon her lap. She then agrees. Then, Hamlet asks her, "Did you think I meant country matters?" Well, clearly this is a pun to make people laugh. It has a double meaning, both country as in uncivilized, and cunt-ry referring to a vagina. He then adds "Tis a fair thought to lie between maids' legs." This probably also got a laugh.

Right up until the early 1600s, there was still no taboo against using blunt language, calling shit shit and fuck fuck. But the groundwork was already laid in the Renaissance. Already, Shakespeare's little pun on the word cunt probably caused people to blush and giggle. A century or more earlier, they wouldn't have even batted an eye at such a comment. But, what was about to happen next would greatly intensify the shamefulness of dirty words.

Chapter 4
Rise of the Bourgeoisie Class

It was at the end of the Renaissance and the beginning of the 17th century that something else was also beginning to happen, something that would cement the social status of Saxon dirty words forever. It was at this time that there became a new class in society. Remember that in the early Middle Ages, there were only two classes, nobles and peasants. But that began to change at a certain point.

With a rapid expansion in international trade, there was also a rise of a wealthy and powerful merchant class in Medieval England. From the 1500s through to the 1800s a large number of European and English merchant import/export companies were formed to exploit new international trading opportunities.

Even by the start of the 17th century, goods usually were transported over fairly short distances, 70 miles at the most. But in the following years, trade routes to Asia and the New World opened up. It was at this time that goods began to be imported from very long distances.

For instance, tea, silk, and porcelain were imported from China. Then, sugar, tobacco, coffee, and rum were imported from the New World. And, calico and spices were imported from India. This had the effect of creating this new social class in England and elsewhere, the merchant class, later referred to as the Bourgeoisie class (pronounced Boor-zhwaa-zee).

At that time, the Bourgeoisie were considered an emerging middle class, but they were actually more wealthy than what we think of as middle class today. They were in between; they were not peasants but not upper class either. Though they were rich, they were not from noble families. They were usually low-born, with their ancestors being tradesmen, servants, workers, and peasants. So, what happens when you have a group of very rich and powerful peasants? They're not noblemen, but they may be as rich or richer than the noble families.

They would often buy nice houses or estates that were formerly owned by Dukes, Lords, and Ladies. The nobility of England would be their neighbors. This raised a lot of questions. What are they, noblemen or peasants? And more importantly, who do they associate with?

Just as we would not expect Bill Gates to be a regular at the local bowling alley, or Donald Trump to hang out in a dive bar in New Jersey, the emerging merchant class of the 17th century sought to socialize with their fellow wealthy Englishmen. The problem was that the other wealthy people were mostly high-born, meaning that they were at least partially noble by birth. And, nobility is not just about blood or DNA; it's more than that. Nobility refers to one's breading, and that has as much or more to do with culture and upbringing as it does genetics.

Breading means knowing how to talk, how to walk, which fork to use with your salad, which spoon to use with your soup, and so on. It also means being well educated. Wealthy young ladies had private tutors, studied music and the arts, while young men from the upper class went to prep schools such as Eton, and then to Universities such as Oxford or Cambridge.

Now remember how there were two different forms of English at that time, proper English and common English? Proper English was spoken by the wealthy and well educated, who were mostly from aristocratic families of Norman descent.

Common English, on the other hand, was spoken by the peasant class, mostly of Anglo-Saxon, Germanic, or Norse descent. You could probably talk to a person for less than half a minute and know exactly what social class they belonged to.

So, what do you think happened when the wealthy but low-born merchants were trying to hob-nob with the wealthy noblemen of the 1600s and 1700s? It was likely a very awkward situation. There was also a reverse situation at this time. Well-bred Englishmen, descended from aristocracy, often lost their family fortunes over several generations due to gambling or poor investments. So, while wealth usually indicated a person's station in life, it was at this time that a wealthy merchant might actually be intimidated by meeting someone who was financially poor but well-bred and well educated.

It was this upwardly mobile Bourgeoisie class that more than anything else cemented the fate of common Middle English obscenities. You see it was this emerging middle class, trying to fit in with their well-bred neighbors that caused them to choose their words more carefully. They normally spoke common English, but they didn't want to appear low class. So, they had to learn what words were proper and what words would be an embarrassment.

We don't know exactly how these situations unfolded, but we can surmise that there were many awkward situations when a wealthy merchant or his wife, who was born a peasant, unthinkingly said shit,

fuck, or cunt in the presence of well-bred nobility.
If there were ladies present, they might gasp and ask
to be excused. The well-mannered gentry might look
at this rich merchant and his wife as nothing more
than glorified servants, overgrown gutter snipes with
a pocket full of cash, nothing more. There must have
been many such situations like this.

We can pretty much piece together what happened
next. Suddenly, for the first time in the English language, these merchants and their families got it into
their heads that certain common words of Germanic
origin were downright shameful. This had never been
an issue before since masters and servants didn't really
socialize as equals.

Previously, the servants could say whatever they
wanted to each other, and their masters talked

amongst themselves. If a servant ever spoke Germanic obscenities in front of their master, it was probably ignored, or viewed as peasant talk, nothing more.

Now that they were co-mingling, the Bourgeoisie families had to quickly get up to speed on what to say or not say, in order to fit in and be accepted by the upper class. Soon, even maids and workmen had to watch their language around their masters, for fear of being perceived as crude or ignorant.

We can only assume that this generalized beyond the merchant class to those one rung below them on the social scale. There must have been conversations between commoners where the richer of the two admonished the other for using obscenities.

You can imagine how it went. Something like this: "You're not supposed to say 'shit', Joe. Don't you know that? It's uncouth! You're supposed to say 'defecashawn'. That's the proper term." These taboos would then spread like a virus among the emerging middle class.

This movement toward increased taboos was then intensified with the Reformation. The Baptists and Puritans were far more-strict. And, as England was engulfed in a Civil War during the 1600s, the royals' indiscretions, previously tolerated, became sinful. Eventually the King himself was executed by the mostly Puritan Parliament. They were so strict that even celebrating a traditional Christmas was banned.

Imagine what would happen if you were caught speaking profanity in public, or if you were drunk and going on an obscene rant. You would probably be put in stocks for sure, and possibly whipped.

No one was safe from condemnation. Sinful acts and language were illegal and punished with corporal punishment. You could be put in the stocks and whipped for things that were openly tolerated just one century earlier. This was even more true in America, a country founded by Puritan pilgrims, where witch hunts became a common occurrence. In the Salem witch trial alone, 19 innocent people were executed.

Then, very much as the upper-class speech and lower-class speech were passed down from generation to generation, so too was this new hybrid Bourgeoisie speech, with all its new taboos. Each generation probably raised their children not to say certain words. But it wasn't just obscenities that became taboo; it was common English that became taboo for all but the lower class, and eventually just being common became taboo.

Chapter 5

Victorian Prudishness

By the 1800s, what began as a small, wealthy group of Bourgeoisie families had morphed into a large and vibrant middle class. Likewise, what began with the Bourgeoisie trying to fit in with high society had become 'middle class values'. This was the age of Queen Victoria, and a new age of strict morality and public decorum had taken over English culture, echoing the Puritan movement of the 1600s

What began as a desire among common folk to not look so common and to fit in with their betters became strict rules of polite society among the English people. And, this was more-true in America than England. Americans began calling their spigots by the French term, 'faucets', while in England they still used the common Saxon term, 'cock'.

At this point, the process that began with the Norman Conquest was complete. Finally, just being a common Saxon came to be seen as obscene and immoral. In fact, being common was the worst thing you could possibly say about someone. In the 1800s being called common was like being slapped in the face. This was taking classism to an ugly extreme but, worse, it was racist because it was only the Saxon, Norse, and Germanic words that were seen as especially common.

The really fascinating thing is that it wasn't just obscene words that developed a negative association. For instance, in Old English if you wanted to say 'scent', you would say 'stench'. It did not originally refer to a foul or unpleasant odor. It was merely the common word for scent or aroma. In fact, they might say something like, "I love your perfume. It has a nice stench."

So how did the Old English word for scent become so negative in the Victorian era? Just like the other dirty words, the word 'stench' was part of the vocabulary of the common people, the Saxons and the Germanic people of England. So, by association, it took on a negative connotation. The words 'scent' and 'aroma', on the other hand, come from French. Do you see the pattern? Saxon bad, French good.

The same thing happened for the word lewd. In the Middle Ages, the Old English word for 'common' was 'lewd'. The word lewd specifically meant non-clergy, or non-professional, or what we call 'lay'. So, if you were referring to a common man you would call him a lewd man. An average house would be described as a lewd house. But, by the 1800's, being common was considered crude and unacceptable in polite society. This is when lewd became *lewd*. And many common Saxon words became lewd words.

This was like Stockholm Syndrome, in which people who are kidnapped begin to identify with their captors. Note that at this time it was not the French nobility outlawing common Saxon words. No. It was the descendants of the common Saxons themselves. True, it did stem from a prejudice against Saxons by the Normans, but that was many centuries earlier. Now it was the Saxons themselves who were embarrassed by their crude Saxon language and preferred to use French or Latin words to sound more-classy.

By the 19th century, common Saxon terms for private parts and private acts became the most offensive words in the English language. This was the peak of prudishness. The 1800s saw the apogee of the rise of civility that began in the Renaissance. This was so extreme that eventually even French and Latin were deemed too blunt. This was an age of euphemisms. They would say things like ineffables, or unmentionables, when referring to something as innocent as women's underwear.

Eventually, just being poor, having a penis or vagina, or having to go to the bathroom all became obscene topics of conversation. It was as if just being human was obscene. And, in a sense this was true. Remember the role of the Reformation and Puritan sensibilities in all of this. To be obscene was to be immoral and, according to Christian theology, we are all sinners. Because of the concept of original sin, just being human was, in a way, obscene.

This was greatly aided by a kind of war on the poor promoted by the robber barons of the 19th century and many influential Protestant leaders. There was a conservative belief at that time that rich people were good people, and commoners were not. They believed that if you were rich it was because you were smarter, worked harder, and were more moral than other people. The rich were blessed by God.

Conversely, if you were poor, you must have done something wrong; you were either lazy or drank too much, or were cursed by God for your immorality. An echo of this belief system still survives to this day in modern conservative political beliefs.

This did not just pertain to language. This was a political, religious, cultural, and social movement, especially in England and the United States. In America, being 'common' was synonymous with being immoral. It was often seen as downright sinful, and deserving of being punished. Is it any wonder that obscenity laws were passed and rigidly enforced? To say that people were strict is an understatement.

But, while England and America were going through the Victorian era, people in Italy, Spain, and France continued to be somewhat more grounded, and one might even say earthy.

If you think about it, our laws against dirty words are a direct extension of the Puritans putting people in stocks and whipping them for their immorality. It's really no different. It is the English version of Sharia Law.

Chapter 6

The 20th century & the FCC

In the 20th century, people embraced science and modernity, and they challenged old taboos. In the 1920s, women wore mini-skirts, danced the Charleston, and drank whiskey and gin in illegal speakeasies. If the Victorian era was characterized by moral strictness and decorum, the 20th Century was an era of fun and frivolity. Among the younger generation especially, and even some older folks, it was considered ok to let your hair down sometimes, and have a little fun.

At this time, people began to think that going to the bathroom, cleaning your genitals, and using proper birth control were matters of science and hygiene, not obscenities. So, it is inevitable that you'll have to talk about them somehow. You can't keep saying 'unmentionables' for everything. So, what did they do?

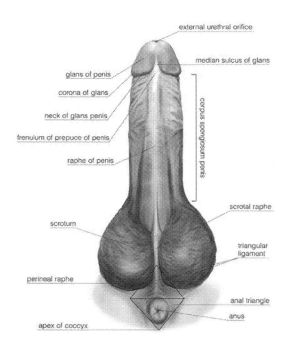

The answer should not surprise you. When doctors, academics, and authors of the 20th century sought to move beyond the silliness of words like 'unmentionables', they invariably turned to words of French or Latin origin. After all, you can't say shit but you can say defecation. You can't say fuck but you can say fornication. Instead of cunt, you can certainly say vagina, vulva or, of course, female genitalia.

They used words of either French or Latin origin, of course, because they were seen as more proper, and thus not so lewd or obscene.

This was the last step in a process that had taken nearly 900 years to complete. For a while, during the 1800s, even French or Latin words for obscene topics were considered too lewd to be spoken aloud in mixed company. But now, in the 20th century, we saw the final step of this long progression toward our modern dirty words. Finally, it was ok to say almost any synonym for defecation, as long as you did not use the Saxon word shit. And, the same was true for all other dirty words of Germanic origin. And, in the early 20th century, this was even true for words that were not so dirty.

We already mentioned that the Saxon word stench, meaning aroma, and lewd, meaning common, had taken on decidedly negative connotations. But, other words suffered a similar fate. This includes words that we don't currently think of as being immoral or very obscene. Yet, even now they are still not considered proper, and saying them often provokes some giggles, if not being downright offensive. In the first half of the 20th century, you could say passing gas but you would never want to use the Germanic word fart in polite company.

Likewise, you could say derrière, but you would never want to use the Saxon word butt, as that was considered too crude and common. And, the word ass, coming from the common Saxon word arse, was just as bad if not worse. And these are just a short list of common Saxon words that had been more or less officially banned from polite conversation, while their French and Latin synonyms were now starting to be widely used in 20th century speech and writing.

By far the biggest change in the 20th century came about when the government took it upon themselves to begin censoring people's public speech in movies, and on broadcast radio. Many states and cities began passing obscenity ordinances to censor films that were judged immoral or obscene. The first of which was in 1907, in Chicago. Believe it or not it was the Chicago police chief that was tasked with screening all films shown in the city. Films deemed to be too lewd for the public were officially banned.

This progressed over the next few decades, and in the 1930s there was a serious crack down on lewdness in films. This eventually resulted in the Production Code Administration (PCA). This was not a government organization but an effort by the Motion Picture Association to prevent government interference.

The industry leaders would agree to regulate themselves to avoid burdensome regulations. In 1934, the PCA passed a rule that all films would have to be screened for obscene and immoral content before being able to be commercially released. While the movie industry opted for self-regulation to avoid government interference, they still imposed penalties for breaking the code.

Even though these codes were enforced to address issues of immorality and lewd conduct on film, the anti-Saxon prejudice was clearly present. For instance, in 1939 David Selznick, the producer of Gone with the Wind, got a slap on the wrist (a $5000 fine) for using the phrase "Frankly my dear, I don't give a damn." in his movie.

If the line had been "I don't give a shit" the film would have been completely banned and the fine much higher. Not surprisingly, 'damn' is of Old French origin, and originally from Latin, while 'shit' is of Saxon origin. So, the ancient prejudice against common Saxon words has now become codified into law, with penalties and fines.

To regulate obscenities on radio, the federal government established the Federal Communications Commission (FCC). The FCC was founded in 1934, and FCC obscenity laws soon followed. The radio producers had to follow a strict code of content to avoid fines and even jail-time. When TV was developed, the FCC expanded their mandate to include regulating TV content as well. Hence you have the "Seven Words You Can't Say on TV."

It is obviously true that, in the 20th century, there appeared to be a very strong prejudice against vulgar words of Germanic origin. But, how do we know that this specifically dates to the Norman Kings prejudice against the ancient Saxons? By the 20th century, so much time had passed that there might well have been other explanations for this anti-German sentiment. Maybe it was simply due to World War I and

II, in which Germany was our enemy.

After all, the King of England during WWI actually changed his last name, in order to sound less German. George V changed the name of his family from 'Saxe-Coburg-Gotha' to 'Windsor'. So, maybe that's why there was an anti-Germanic bias in our language. But, that's not the case, and we can prove it. You see, we can date the period that the prejudice against Germanic words occurred in our language.

Dating the Prejudice

We can date our prejudice against words of Germanic origin because there is no such discrimination against modern German words. For instance, it is perfectly ok to say fick, schista, scheide, or schwans on American broadcast TV or Radio. Even though all of those words are Germanic in origin, none of them are specifically banned. Why are some Germanic words ok and others are banned? Fick is ok but fuck is not, even though they both mean the same thing. Likewise, schista is ok but shit is not, even though they mean the same thing as well.

We can say scheide but not cunt, though they mean the same thing. And, schwans is ok but cock is not, even though they mean the exact same thing. Why? The answer is extremely revealing. Fick, schista, scheide and schwans are all modern German words. Whereas, fuck, shit, cunt and cock are all very old, from Middle English or before. All these words date from the 11th to the 14th centuries.

This is very interesting because it means that we can date the origin of this anti-Germanic prejudice. And what is that date? It is the period from the Norman Conquest to the Renaissance. This is the time of Robin Hood, the period of the Norman, Plantagenet, and Tudor Kings. In other words, this could not be a modern or recent anti-German prejudice. It is really a very ancient anti-Saxon prejudice, specifically perpetuated at the time of the ancient Normans' occupation and oppression of the Saxon peasants.

It turns out that we only have a prejudice against truly ancient Middle English words, this also includes words from Old English, Middle Dutch, Old High German, and Old Norse. But, we have no such ban on words from modern Germanic or Norse languages such as German, Dutch, Danish or Swedish.

As bizarre as it sounds, it is literally only Germanic words that were commonly used from the 11th to the 14th centuries that we cannot say on TV today. How bizarre is that? Furthermore, we even define these words as being 'lewd', which in Old English originally just meant common and ordinary words.

Obscenity Arrests & Fines

None of this would be important nor worthy of publishing a book about if it were not for the very real laws, fines, arrests, and other government actions taken in the 20th century to control the use of dirty words. The entire topic is really somewhat silly, slightly titillating, and usually giggle-worthy, until we look at the lives that have been potentially ruined by this 1000-year old racial prejudice.

In the second half of the 20th century, some brave citizens have sought to challenge the government's ability to limit free speech. They have publicly ridiculed our ban on so-called 'dirty words'. They have pointed out the very issue that I raised at the outset of this book. Why is it that we can say crap but not shit? We can say vagina but not cunt. We can say fornicate but not fuck. What is it about these words that is so toxic to people? Some simply argue that it is a matter of free speech and should not be something that the government is able to regulate.

Three people, in particular, have challenged our FCC and local obscenity laws and taken these cases to Court. All three of these people were comedians or performers. Lenny Bruce, George Carlin, and Howard Stern have all wrestled with either local obscenity laws, or the FCC or both, and for the most part they have won in the end. As a result, the way the FCC and other government agencies enforce these laws have changed somewhat, and the list of banned words has, at least, shrunk a bit. What follows is a summary of their legal battles.

Lenny Bruce

The comedian Lenny Bruce was first arrested on October 4, 1961, for obscenity at the Jazz Workshop in San Francisco. He had used the word cocksucker in a comedy routine. The jury acquitted him but, after that, law enforcement agencies more closely monitored his appearances, which resulted in more frequent arrests under existing obscenity laws.

Bruce was then arrested at the Gate of Horn folk club in Chicago on December 5, 1962. Soon after this he played at The Establishment Club in London, and the next year the British government had barred him from entering England as an "undesirable alien".

Lenny Bruce

Bruce was arrested again in 1963 in Los Angeles, California. The arresting officer was a young man named Sherman Block who would later become the LA County Sheriff. He was charged with obscenity for using the word schmuck, which nowadays just means a stupid person, but it was originally a Yiddish term that means penis. Can you imagine being arrested today for saying schmuck?

Finally, he appeared twice at the Café Au Go Go in Greenwich Village in 1964, with undercover police detectives in the audience. He was arrested along with the club owners, Howard and Elly Solomon, and they were charged with public obscenity. On both occasions, the charges were again because of his use of various dirty words.

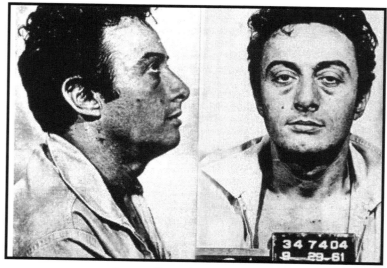

Lenny Bruce's Arrest Photo

The trial lasted six months. A three-judge panel presided over the widely publicized trial. During the trial a number of notable figures came forward in Bruce's defense, among them, Woody Allen, Bob Dylan, Allen Ginsberg, Norman Mailer, Jules Feiffer, and sociologist Herbert Gans. But, on November 4, 1964, Bruce and club owner Howard Solomon were both found guilty of obscenity.

On December 21, 1964, Bruce was sentenced to four months of hard labor. He was later set free on bail during the appeals process, but died before the appeal was decided. Solomon's conviction was later overturned on appeal. Later, the Governor gave Bruce a full pardon, after his death.

George Carlin

In the early 1970's George Carlin picked up where Lenny Bruce had left off, with his best-known routine, "Seven Words You Can Never Say on Television," which first appeared on his comedy album, "Class Clown". This was not subjected to FCC laws, but when he performed it on stage, he was subject to local obscenity laws.

George Carlin

Carlin was arrested after performing his "Seven Words" routine at Milwaukee's Summerfest and charged with violating obscenity laws in 1972. Carlin then referred to the words as "the Milwaukee Seven". The case was dismissed in the same year; the judge declared that the language was indecent, but Carlin did have the right to say it, as long as he caused no disturbance.

In 1973, a man complained to the FCC after his young son heard a similar routine, "Filthy Words", from his album, "Occupation: Foole", which was broadcast over WBAI FM, in New York City. The station owner, Pacifica, received a citation from the FCC, for broadcasting obscene material. This lead to a lengthy legal challenge that lasted years and went all the way to the U.S. Supreme Court.

US Supreme Court

The Supreme Court, in 1978, upheld the FCC's authority to fine broadcasters for saying dirty words at hours when children could be listening. In a 5 to 4 vote, the U.S. Supreme Court supported the FCC action, and they ruled that the routine was indecent and that the FCC had authority to prohibit such broadcasts (F.C.C. v. Pacifica Foundation, 438 U.S. 726.).

The matter was settled. And, between 1975 and 1987, no television or radio broadcaster dared to use obscenities. But, that was before Howard Stern.

Howard Stern

Howard Stern was a brazenly brash shock jock from the late 1970's, who pioneered a new type of comedy radio show. He used the same kind of language that Bruce and Carlin had, but he had the audacity to do it on broadcast radio. This ended up being arguably the biggest obscenity case in history. The FCC, from 1990 to 2004, issued fines totaling $2.5 million to broadcast radio stations for airing The Howard Stern Show, the highest amount of any American radio show.

The Supreme Court had provided broadcasting guidelines for indecent material in its 1978 ruling. They specifically forbade the 'seven dirty words' made famous by comedian George Carlin. The FCC had received complaints about Howard Stern as early as

1981 when he was at WWDC in Washington D.C., but due to stipulations in the Communications Act of 1934 and First Amendment laws, they were limited in their power to control his freedom of speech.

Howard Stern on the cover of Rolling Stone

In 1985 Stern had relocated to WNBC in New York City. And, the complaints to the FCC about Stern continued and increased. The FCC responded, "Our role in overseeing program content is...very limited...the First Amendment protects the right of broadcasters to air statements which may be offensive, and a free society requires governmental forbearance in those instances." Finally, the FCC decided to address this issue by changing their guidelines to crack down on Stern's blatant use of indecent content. In 1987, after an investigation of The Howard Stern Show, the FCC broadened its guidelines.

At this point, Stern was broadcasting at WXRK in New York owned by Infinity Broadcasting. And, in 1990, Infinity Broadcasting, the owner of Stern's flagship station WXRK, and some of his syndication affiliates were issued fines. Then, two penalties issued in 1992 worth $105,000 and $600,000 respectively were the highest the agency had fined any broadcaster. Further violations led to almost $2 million in fines being issued by the end of 1994. A settlement reached between the FCC and Infinity in 1995 included a 1.715 million dollar payment to dismiss all outstanding indecency cases.

But, Stern continued to receive fines from the FCC. And, in 2004, Stern announced his departure from terrestrial radio to begin a five-year contract with Sirius Satellite Radio, a subscription-based radio service, exempt from FCC regulation. The Howard Stern Show aired for the last time on broadcast radio on December 16, 2005.

Bruce, Carlin, and Stern were not the only people arrested for violating obscenity laws. The writer, Allen Ginsgerg, had his book "Howl" confiscated by U.S. Customs officials in 1955, declaring that it was obscene. That was challenged in court and overturned, based on the constitutional right to free speech.

There have been many others arrested for obscenity. The early film actress, Mae West, was arrested for writing a play called *Sex*. And, the rap group 2-Live-Crew were arrested for recording a song with racy lyrics. Many others have been arrested for lewd acts or images. They include Hugh Hefner, Jim Morrison, and Wendy O. Williams, among others.

Conclusion

By the year 2019, of the original seven words, only three words are really prosecuted by the FCC; fuck, shit, and cunt. Of course, any and all synonyms are acceptable, and are routinely used without any fine or condemnation by the FCC, including screw, crap, beaver, and any other crude slang you can think of. Nearly 1000 years after the Norman conquest, there is still a very short list of common but ancient Saxon and Germanic words that are banned by our government today.

In an era of artificial intelligence, at a time when we are seriously talking about colonies on the moon and on Mars, you can still be fined and arrested for publicly speaking ancient, common Saxon words.

Chapter 7
The Final Word

So now you know the history behind how these words became so dirty and forbidden in our language. Now, let's examine these words a little more closely. We'll look at their etymology, and the current justification for keeping them labled as 'dirty'. And, in addition to the seven words mentioned so far, I have a few more of my own.

While Lenny Bruce and George Carlin came up with their own words you can't say on TV, I have come up with my own list of 19 words that are either obscene or at least negative, based on the Norman prejudice against Saxons and their language. Bruce and Carlin identified: Shit, Fuck, Cunt, Motherfucker, Cocksucker, Tits, and Piss. These are the first seven words on the my list of 19 common Saxon words.

These are all very funny to say, but if we want to get serious about this list there are some changes we need to make. First, you have Fuck and Motherfucker on the same list. Isn't that a bit redundant? Do we need to list every possible usage of the word Fuck? The same is true for Cock. Is it ok to say "he had a big cock", but it's not ok to say "he was a cocksucker"? No. This totally redundant. We really only need to list Cock, and not any other specific usage of the word.

Current Word	Original Word	Origin	Definition
1. Shit	Scite	Old English	Defecate
2. Fuck	Fyck	Germanic/Norse	Fornicate
3. Cunt	Kunte	Germanic/Norse	Vagina
4. Motherfucker	Mothir Fycker	Germanic/Norse	Maternal Fornicator
5. Cocksucker	Cocc Sucan	Old English	Oral Sex
6. Tits	Tittr	Old English	Mammary Glands
7. Piss	Pissier	Old French	Urinate
8. Cock	Cocc	Old English	Male Bird (Penis)
9. Fart	Ferzan	Old German	To Exit (Pass Gas)
10. Dick	Dicke	Old German	Big, Fat & Thick, (Penis)
11. Bitch	Bicce	Old English	Female Dog
12. Butt	Buttuc	Old English	Posterior
13. Ass	Arse	Old English	Posterior
14. Slut	Schlutt	Old German	Slovenly Woman
15. Whore	Hore	Old English	Prostitute or Promiscuous
16. Bollocks	Beallucas	Old English	Testicles
17. Suck	Sucan	Old English	To Draw by Suction
18. Stench	Stenc	Old English	Aroma
19. Lewd	laewde	Old English	Common, Ordinary

Note that almost all the words on the list were used by the ancient Saxons in Middle English. But, there was one exception among Carlin's 7 words. One vulgar word, Piss, actually comes from a French word. Piss is from the Old French word Pissier. This is from the vulgar Latin word Pisiare. So, clearly this is the proverbial "execption that proves the rule". But, you may note that piss is not nearly as shocking as using the words fuck or cunt, and nowadays you can even say piss on broadcast media. So, even among vulgarities, there's a bias against words of Germanic origin.

There are, however, a few Saxon words that were not on George Carlin's list. And, those are dick, bitch, fart, butt and ass. Now some might say that fart is not so bad. But, it is nonetheless somehow cruder than saying passing gas, which is a distinctly French way of saying the same thing. Dick and ass are also both considered crude. Of course, they mean the same thing as Penis and Derriére, which are publicly acceptable because they come from either French or Latin. Butt and bitch have almost become acceptable English, though they're still considered crude.

Other words that I added include slut, whore, bollocks, suck, stench, and lewd, because they were all common words with innocent meanings that have become negative only because they are Old English words used by Saxon commoners.

So, now we have our list of Saxon vulgarisms. You will note on the list above that 12 of the 19 are from Old English, the language of the Saxon peasants at the time of the Norman Conquest.

Another three words are from Old German. We know that the original Saxon language was an ancient German dialect. Therefore, it's likely that these words were known and spoken by the ancient Saxons, even if they were not written down until the time of Middle English.

Another 3 words are listed as having a Germanic/ Norse origin. That is because, as you will see, variations of these words are found in multiple ancient languages, usually Old Norse and Old German, or Middle German. Since, we can't pinpoint the main source of the word, we just say it's of Germanic/Norse origin.

Some people have argued that only some of these words originate with ancient Anglo-Saxons, while others come from Old Norse, Old German, Middle

German, Old Dutch or some other ancient language, including one from Old French. But this is a red herring because all these words, except one, are of Germanic origin, including words from Old English. Likewise, all the proper words in English also appear to come from a common source, and that is Old French and/or Latin.

More than anything else, the one point that I hope people take away from an examination of these words is that the English Language is principally made up of two earlier language groups. One group is all of the Germanic and Norse languages of Northern Europe. The other group is made up of Old French, and much of these words originated in ancient Latin.

When we look at the dichotomy of proper words vs. dirty words in the English language, the lists are mutually exclusive. Almost all proper words come from the French/Latin language group. And, almost every single dirty word comes from the Germanic Language group, especially Old English words spoken by the ancient Anglo-Saxons. When we look at this stark dichotomy in the English language, the argument that dirty words actually come from a variety of languages just doesn't hold true.

In this dichotomy of English words, we see that at the root of this split is the cultural clash between the Norman upper class, using Old French and Latin words, vs. the common Saxon peasants, who were essentially a Germanic people, using words from Germanic and Norse origins. It was this general clash between Germanic and French culture that lies at the heart of our bias against dirty words today. Lewd words were literally just common Saxon words.

Summary

Looking at all the research we've uncovered in this book, the results are clear. If you want proof that it was the Norman Conquest that made Saxon dirty words taboo, just look at our current culture and laws. The word poop is not very polite, but it's not illegal, nor is it seen as extremely nasty. The same is true for boobs, shagging, boffing, or BJ's. These words mean exactly the same thing as shit, tits, fucking, and cocksucking, so they should be just as nasty as but they are clearly deemed by society to be very different. Why?

Why is one synonym so much worse that another? Why is it ok to say that "she had big boobs" and "they were shagging all night long," but you cannot say the exact same thing using Saxon words? And, the only difference between these words is the historical origin of the words. Every other synonym originating in modern English or other languages is ok to say in public. But, not ancient Saxon. Ancient Germanic words alone are forbidden, and worse, it's even illegal.

Our societal outrage at these particular Saxon dirty words reveals something like an ancient scar on our culture, passed down generation after generation.

Why else would the word cunt or fuck be so incredibly bad that you can be fined or jailed for saying it? But you can say beaver or boff, and no one cares. And the proper terms to use on TV or Radio are all either Latin or French, such as vagina, penis, defecate, or copulate.

There is only one reason why these words could be deemed so horrible, and that is because, just as now, after the Norman conquest these words must have been considered crude, and the use of them must have been harshly judged and even punished. People using these words in court or in the presence of a Norman Lady may have been blinded, or had their tongues cut out, or worse, execution by torture. These were common punishments often for even petty crimes. Norman brutality in Medieval times was barbaric and swift.

Likewise, it is no coincidence that the proper and acceptable words to be used in public, and on TV or Radio, are all either Latin or French. Latin makes some sense, I guess, since all of Europe was once part of the Roman Empire, and later the Holy Roman Empire. But, why French? Why are those words so much better than Saxon? Clearly, this must be for no reason other than the Norman Conquest.

Let's go back and review the steps that led to our current situation. Here we have a culmination of hundreds of years of events combining to create our modern dirty words. The following is a brief culmination of the events listed in this book that resulted in our current bifurcated list of words for obscene topics.

A Brief Chronology of English Lewd Words:

1. In the beginning there was the Germanic, Anglo-Saxon language, called Ænglish. All of our modern dirty words were just common Germanic words at that time.

2. The Norman conquest was followed by prejudice and oppression against Saxons, and this created a class system reflected in language. Normans spoke a French dialect, and the Saxons spoke a German dialect called Old English.

3. Renaissance culture made private parts and private acts strictly private, hence referring to such things was made increasingly inappropriate in polite company.

4. Starting in the 1600s, the Bourgeoisie, the emerging middle class, desperately wanted to fit in with the Norman upper class and not appear so common or lewd, so they used proper language to differentiate themselves from the crude commoners.

5. Eventually lewd language, which just meant the common language, became 'lewd', meaning obscene or indecent. And, the definition of lewd, meaning 'common', actually became an extinct definition of the word.

6. This peaked in the 1800s when any private thing was taboo to talk about in any language, especially if ladies were present. This was especially true in America.

7. Finally, in the modern scientific world, now that the silly prudishness of the 1800s has been shaken off, we can once again refer to these indiscrete topics in public. And, when we want to refer to unmentionables, we use French or Latin, of course, because it has already been established in the English language that French and Latin are proper but lewd Germanic words are, well, 'lewd'.

8. In the 20th century, FCC anti-obscenity laws were enacted and enforced. Stiff fines and imprisonment were the consequences of speaking Saxon. Hence, Lenny Bruce and George Carlin, and later Howard Stern had their legal problems. And, of course Carlin's list of seven words you can't say on television were almost all words of Old Saxon, Germanic or Norse origin.

9. In spite of significant progress in our culture at large, very little difference is seen in mainstream broadcast TV, radio, and print media, even to this day, especially regarding the big 3: Fuck, Shit, and Cunt.

10. Conclusion: Our FCC laws are actually enforcing a 1000-year old Norman prejudice against Saxons, with huge fines or imprisonment. It's racism and classism, pure and simple.

Conclusion:

My Self-Righteous Rant

Nowadays, people are more permissive and can talk about anything in public. Ironically, it's only the ban on Ancient Saxon that continues. But, it's not the Normans who are doing it now. It's us. We don't want our children to learn these Saxon words and we teach them it's ok to say other words that mean the same things, so long as they don't speak Saxon. So, the prejudice against ancient Saxon and Germanic words continues and we ourselves are perpetuating it.

Surely, the reason why we can say copulate or fornicate but not say fuck is nothing more than anti-Saxon prejudice. We just have to remember that for 400 years after the Norman Conquest the official language of England was a dialect of French, and this helped to shape the modern English language. So now, with very few exceptions, English words of French origin are deemed proper, and words meaning the exact same thing but coming from a Saxon, Norse, or Germanic origin are deemed vulgar.

It is unbelievable that you can use almost any synonym you can think of for shit, cunt, or fuck, and it's perfectly ok; it is no problem at all, so long as you use a non-Saxon synonym. But, if you use these very Saxon/Germanic words on broadcast TV or radio, you can be fined hundreds of thousands of dollars, even to this very day.

There are plenty of non-Saxon slang words we can use on the radio or TV without fines and punishment, even when they describe the same crude things. We can say poop, poopy, pee-pee, wee-wee, T&A, buns, tah-tahs, boffing, shagging, getting it on, humping, and so on. None of these words are the Queen's proper English, and all are synonyms for the dirty words. But, alas, they are not Old Saxon words, so they are ok.

Think about that. As long as they are not 1000-year old Germanic words, of course, they are ok. Crazy isn't it?

And some of these dirty words were not even from vulgar German words at all. Some came from Hoch-Deutsch, Old High German, proper German spoken by kings. These are words such as Shit, Fart, and Ass. In fact, you can see the German word for fart, 'abfahrt', on German freeways to this day, it simply means to exit or depart. Yet, these were still frowned upon by the Normans, and their descendants.

And, as mentioned before, the proper Saxon word for common was 'lewd', and the Saxon word for aroma was 'stench'. Surely these are examples of Norman prejudice even if the other words are not.

The truth is that our dirty words are really not dirty words at all, they are really just common Old English and other common Germanic words. They are words that 1000 years ago were perfectly okay to say in public. In Middle English, there was no other common word for vagina, other than cunt. Cunt was the proper term. Just as shit was the proper term for defecation.

Fuck was used to mean rubbing together or striking back and forth quickly. And, later it came to mean sex. Even then, it was just a common term for fornication. They may have been considered crude or distasteful words to the delicate Norman nobility, but these were not considered obscene words among the common people of England; it was just the common words of their language.

The acts may be obscene, thus any word used to describe them are obscene, but there is no difference between fornicate and fuck, other than Norman prejudice against Saxons. This prejudice has been so indoctrinated in the English people that they adopted these same prejudices themselves; French is noble, Saxon is crude and common. Now the English speaking peoples' shame of their own Saxon origins is baked into the cake of the English language.

Let's think about this. Can you imagine another racial group being treated this way? Can you imagine a world in which Caucasian slang words used for defecation and fornication are perfectly ok to say on the radio or on TV, but African American slang words are considered dirty and vulgar, and you will be fined and arrested for saying them? Can you imagine the uproar if conservative legislators in the South passed such a law today, declaring Caucasian obscenities okay but African American slang DIRTY and ILLEGAL? How long would those laws last? But that's exactly what we do every day with Saxon words!

And, the really odd part is that the English Saxons don't even exist anymore as a distinct group. It's not like they have separate bathrooms in England for the Normans and Saxons. These feuds ended hundreds and hundreds of years ago.

What was originally racism against the Saxons then became classism, looking down on the crude and common peasants. Eventually, those classist values permeated our culture. Nowadays, we no longer even know where our bias against these dirty words came from.

You'd have to go back to the days of Robin Hood to find evidence of widespread anti-Saxon prejudice. Yet, our U.S. government has seen fit to continue its fight against the lewd and common Saxon language to this very day.

Now that you know the story, if you are going to blame any one person for our silly laws against dirty words, it would probably be William the Bastard, architect of the Norman Conquest. This is the Curse of William the Bastard.

And, in case you were wondering, as far as I can tell from my genealogy research, I am from both Norman and German ancestry. But, I can't help but feel for the poor Saxons who, to a great extent, gave us our language, dirty words and all. Long live the Heathen Saxon Horde!

Appendix:
A Dictionary of Lewd Words

And now, I present the following annotated dictionary of Saxon words, still used in English today. This is based upon a number of dictionaries, especially the Oxford English Dictionary, Webster's Unabridged Dictionary, and Dictionary.com. Note that I include a couple of vulgar definitions for each word, but there are, of course, many other usages. Many of these words can be used as a noun, verb, or adverb. Piss has been omitted, as it is French.

The point of this glossary is really to show the history and origin of each of these words. More than anything, this is the research that clearly shows how all of our current dirty words are almost exclusively from Anglo-Saxon, Germanic and/or Norse origin. Meanwhile, you can look up their acceptable and proper synonyms and you will see that they are all from Old French or Latin.

Dictionary:

Ass: 1. buttocks, 2. rectum, 3. a contemptible person. History: before 11th century; variant of arse, (with loss of r before s, as in passel, cuss, etc.); Middle English ars, er (e) s, Old English ærs, ears; Old Norse, Middle Low German, Old Saxon, Old High German ars (German Arsch).

Bitch: 1. a female dog, 2. a malicious, unpleasant, selfish person, especially a woman, 3. a lewd woman, 4. a submissive person, 5. (verb) to complain, gripe. Before 1000 CE, Middle English bicche; from Old English bicce.

Bollocks: n. 1. male testicles, 2. non-sense. Old English beallucas, diminutive (pl) of beallu.

Butt: n. 1. the base or end of anything, 2. the unused end, "a cigar butt." 3. A cut of pork, 4. slang, buttocks. Old English, buttuc, end.

Cock: 1. a male bird, 2. Penis. History: before 900CE; Middle English cock, Old English cocc; cognate with Old Norse kokkr.

Cunt: 1. vagina, 2. a contemptuous term for a woman. History: 1275-1325CE; Middle English cunte; cognate with Old Norse kunta, Old Frisian, Middle Low German, Middle Dutch, kunte

Dick: 1. penis, 2. detective (older use), 3. a contemptible person. History: The meaning 'penis' is attested from 1891 in Farmer's slang dictionary. But, there is evidence that this word is far older, and of Germanic origin. Coming from Middle Low German, the word dicke means Big, Fat, Thick, and Chunky, and it is still used in modern German. It is clear to see how this word from Middle Low German was likely in common usage among Saxons in Old and Middle English. And, its relationship to a penis is obvious.

Fart: 1. To expel gas; break wind. History: Middle English farten ; related to Old Norse freta, Old High

German ferzan (fértzen) to break wind. In Modern German the word Fahren (conjugated as fahrt) means to exit, to leave, to depart, or to travel. Freeway exits in Germany are marked "Abfahrt", meaning to exit the freeway.

Fuck: 1. sexual intercourse, 2. to treat unfairly or harshly; as in "he really fucked me over on that deal", 3. An exclamation, as in "Oh fuck!", 4. a contemptible person; as in "he's a stupid fuck", and many, many other usages. Likely from Old Norse or Old German, perhaps from Flemmish. Cognate with Norwegian fukka 'copulate', or Swedish dialectal focka "copulate, strike, push".

Cognate to Middle English fyke, also spelled fike "to move restlessly, fidget," probably is from a general North Sea Germanic word; German, ficken, sex. Earlier meaning "to make quick movements to and fro, flick," or "to itch, or scratch;"

Possibly from before the 11th century, the earliest appearance of the current spelling was in 1535 -- "Bischops ... may fuck thair fill and be unmaryit" [from Sir David Lyndesay, "Ane Satyre of the Thrie Estaits"]. In Old English, they had other words for sex, such as 'Swive' or 'Sard'.

Lewd: adj. 1. inclined to or characterized by, or inciting to lust or lechery; lascivious. 2. obscene or indecent. History: before 1100, from Old English laewde, originally meaning layman, or common.

Shit: 1. Excrement; feces, 2. the act of defecating, 3. an exclamation, such as "Oh Shit!", 4. anything that is false, poor in quality, or undesirable, as in "that's a load of shit," 5. anything that is of very good quality, as in "that's some good shit!", and many other usages. History: variant of earlier shite, (with short i from past participle or noun) Middle English shiten, from Old English scītan; compare Middle Low German, Middle Dutch schiten (Dutch schijten), Old High German skīzan (German scheissen); continuation of Old English scite

Slut: n. c.1400, 1. a dirty, slovenly, or untidy woman, Middle English, slutt, probably cognate with dialectal German Schlutt 'slovenly woman,' dialectal Swedish slata "idle woman, slut," and Dutch slodde 'slut,' slodder 'a careless man,' Chaucer uses "sluttish" (late 1300s.) in reference to the appearance of an untidy man.

Stench: 1. fowl odor, stink. Old English stenc; related to Old Saxon, Old High German stank; see stink, originally meaning aroma, or scent.

Suck: v. 1. to draw in by way of suction, "the pump sucked the water out", 2. to draw out with your mouth, "he sucked the juice out with a straw". Old English, sucan, Old Norse, súga.

Tits: 1. female breasts, 2. an animal's teats, recorded before 1100; Middle English titte, Old English titt; cognate with Middle Low German, Middle Dutch titte, German Zitze, Norwegian titta.

Whore: n. 1. a prostitue, 2. a promiscuous person, 3. anyone who prostitutes themselves, sells out their values for money. Before 1100; Old English hōre; cognate with German Hure, Old Norse hōra; akin to Gothic hors, harlot.

Selected Bibliography

Bachman, E. M. (2018). *Literary Obscenities: U.S. Case Law and Naturalism After Modernism.* University Park, PA: Pennsylvania State University Press.

Burchfield, R. (1985). *The English Language.* Oxford: Oxford University Press.

Carpenter, D. (2003). *The Struggle for Mastery, Britain 1066-1284.* London: Penguin Books.

Chibnall, M. (1986). *Anglo-Norman England: 1066-1166.* Oxford: Blackwell Publishers Ltd.

Hunt, M. R. (1996). *The Middling Sort: Commerce, Gender, and the Family in England, 1680-1780.* Berkeley: University of California Press.

Mohr, Melissa. (2016). *Holy Shit: A History of Swearing.* Oxford: Oxford University Press.

Morris, Marc. (2014). *The Norman Conquest: The Battle of Hastings and the Fall of Anglo-Saxon England.* New York: Pegasus Books.

Nennius. (2004) *History of the Britons.* Whitefish, MT: Kessinger Publishing LLC.

Perkin, Harold. (2002). *The Origins of Modern English Society: Second Edition.* London: Routledge, Taylor & Francis Group.

Pyle, Howard. (1883). *The Merry Adventures of Robin Hood: Of Great Renown in Nottinghamshire.* New York: Dover Publications.

Soans, C., & Hawker, S. (2008). *Compact Oxford English Dictionary: of Current English, Third Edition.* Oxford: Oxford University Press.

Stubbs, W. (2018). *Germany in the Early Middle Ages, 476-1250: The History and Lives of the Frankish and Teutonic Kings.* Createspace Independent Publishing Platform.

Time-Life Books (Eds). (1997). *What Life Was Like: In the Age of Chivalry: Medieval Europe AD 800-1500.* New York: Time-Life Inc.

(2003) *Webster's New Universal Unabridged Dictionary: Fully Revised and Updated.* New York: Barnes & Noble.

Welch, M. (1993). *Discovering Anglo-Saxon England.* University Park, PA: Pennsylvania State University Press.

Credits

Index

Romanized Celts, 34
sex, sexual, 45, 50, 87, 97, 101-102
Shakespeare, William, 50-51
shame, 44-46, 49-51
shit, 6-9, 11, 13, 42, 44, 46, 48, 50-51, 56, 59,
    70-73, 75, 77, 86-87, 91, 94-97, 102
social class, 45, 53, 56
stench, 63-64, 71, 87, 89, 96
Stern, Howard, 7-8, 78, 83-85
Supreme Court, 78, 82-83
swearing, 11, 44
television, TV, 7-10, 43, 74-75, 77, 87, 92, 94-97
urinate, 87
vagina, 9, 13, 42, 47, 50, 66, 70, 77, 87, 92, 97, 101,
Victoria, Queen, 62, 64, 68,
Victorian era, 62-69
West, Mae, 86
William the Bastard, aka William the Conqueror,
    26-31, 34, 36, 43
WWI, 75

About the Author

D. W. KREGER

Dr. Kreger is a clinical psychologist, an expert on the occult, and a writer and researcher in the fields of psychology, history, archaeology, and ancient mysticism. He holds a Ph.D. in clinical psychology, completed his post-doctoral training in clinical neuropsychology, and is a Diplomate of the International Academy of Behavioral Medicine, Counseling, and Psychotherapy. In addition to his psychological research, he has investigated archaeological sites in 17 countries around the world.

His work has been presented at major academic conferences, and appeared in both research journals and popular media. He is the author of several books, including The Secret Tao: Uncovering the Hidden History and Meaning of Lao Tzu, and The Tao of Yoda. Currently, he is a writer and consulting clinical psychologist in private practice. He lives with his family on a small vineyard, north of Los Angeles, CA.

Made in the USA
Middletown, DE
21 December 2024

67940182R00066